BRINGING JESUS TO WORK

LEADING WITH FAITH, INTEGRITY, AND PURPOSE

BY MARK THOMPSON

Published in the United States of America by

Spirit Media Publishing and our logos are trademarks of
Spirit Media Inc
205 S Academy Street STE #3251
Cary, NC 27519
1 (888) 800-3744 | https://spiritmedia.us

Religion & Spirituality | Christian Living | Work

Paperback ISBN: 979-8-89307-144-3
eBook ISBN: 979-8-89307-229-7
PDF ISBN: 979-8-89307-231-0
Library of Congress Control Number: 2026902240

TABLE OF CONTENTS

PREFACE: BREAKING DOWN THE FIREWALL OF FAITH

Growing up in a small town, faith was the heartbeat of my childhood—shaped by my mother's unwavering devotion to God and Jesus Christ. Sundays were sacred: church services, Sunday school, and confirmation classes filled our weekends with biblical stories and spiritual rhythms. Yet faith felt confined to those moments. The pastor, cloaked in white robes and preaching from a distant pulpit, seemed as unreachable as God Himself. Faith was a Sunday ritual, rarely spilling into my home, school, or friendships.

This pattern followed me into adulthood. Even as I attended church regularly, faith remained compartmentalized. It was a box I checked on Sunday mornings, not a lens through which I lived. After college, as I entered the workplace and got engaged, my fiancée and I continued attending church—but the firewall persisted. Jesus rarely crossed my mind at work or home. Faith was present, but passive.

Everything shifted when my wife and I moved to North Carolina and joined a vibrant church. Through small groups, we discovered a faith that permeated every aspect of our lives. The shift was in friendships, family, and decisions. We learned to weave God into our daily rhythms, dismantling the barriers I'd grown up with. Yet one frontier remained: the workplace.

As a business coach and Chief Revenue Officer, I worked with immigrant customers and offshore clients across dozens of countries. Their seamless integration of faith into professional life was a revelation. It exposed the firewall I'd unknowingly accepted, where my faith stopped at the office door. Conversations with other Christians echoed this frustration: the business world often silences faith, leaving us unsure how to bridge the gap.

This study was born from that conviction. Drawing on biblical wisdom and practical experience, *Bringing Jesus to Work* equips Christian professionals to break down the firewall between faith and work. It's not about perfection, it's about progress. The goal is to transform your workplace into a mission field, where you live boldly as a witness to God's love and truth.

Through trust, transparency, and transformational relationships, we'll explore how to love our zip code by loving those we work with. This is a call to live a faith without boundaries where Jesus isn't just a Sunday guest, but a constant presence guiding every moment of your professional life.

Matthew 28:19-20 (NIV)

"Therefore go and make disciples of all nations, baptizing them in the name of the Father and of the Son and of the Holy Spirit, and teaching them to obey everything I have commanded you. And surely I am with you always, to the very end of the age."

INTRODUCTION

Bringing Jesus to Work: Leading with Faith, Integrity, and Purpose

Why This Movement Matters

Most Christians don't need another Bible study.

They need a battle plan.

They show up to work every day, leading teams, solving problems, making decisions, but often do it in isolation from their faith. Not because they don't believe, but because no one ever showed them how to lead spiritually in the places where they spend most of their time.

Church taught them how to worship.

Work taught them how to perform.

But no one taught them how to integrate the two.

This guide is for the person who's ready to change that.

It's for the leader who's tired of compartmentalizing their faith.

For the person who wants to lead with integrity, wisdom, and spiritual authority without being preachy, awkward, or irrelevant, this is for you.

It's also for the pastor, chaplain, or ministry leader who's looking for a practical, scalable way to disciple people beyond Sunday.

Whether you're launching this study in your church or leading it in your workplace, this guide is designed to spark transformation one conversation, one relationship, one decision at a time.

The Problem We're Solving

- **Faith feels passive**. People are taught to receive, not lead.

- **Work feels secular.** Faith is often left out of business decisions, team dynamics, and leadership conversations.

- **Church feels disconnected.** Sunday sermons rarely equip people for Monday realities.

The Vision of This Movement

Vision and Purpose

To build a multiplying network of Christians who lead spiritually in their workplaces through authentic relationships, wise decision-making, and intentional discipleship.

This isn't just a book. It's a blueprint, a framework for spiritual leadership that starts with you and multiplies through others.

What You'll Learn

- How to build trust and authenticity in workplace relationships

- How to make wise, faith-driven decisions under pressure

- How to disciple others without being preachy or awkward

- How to start and multiply workplace Christian groups

- How to lead with spiritual authority in secular environments

How It Works

You'll walk through a 10-week framework designed to build spiritual depth, relational trust, and leadership clarity. Each week includes:

- A biblical theme
- Guided discussion questions
- At-work challenges to apply your faith
- Tools to foster transparency, mentorship, and spiritual growth

This is not theory. It's practice.

It's not just inspiration. It's activation.

Your Invitation

God made you unique. You were made for more than quiet faith. You were made to disciple and lead others in Jesus' image.

Whether you're joining a group or leading one, this study is your invitation to bring Jesus to work.

HOW TO USE THIS GUIDE

Whether you're leading a group or joining one, this guide is designed to help you integrate faith into your work life with clarity, courage, and community.

It's built for flexibility. You can use it in a church setting, a workplace lunchroom, a virtual group, or a living room. The format works for pastors discipling staff, business leaders mentoring peers, or small groups of people walking through the study together.

Each week follows a simple rhythm:

Weekly Flow

- Theme & Scripture: A biblical principle tied to real-world leadership and workplace dynamics

- Discussion Questions: Designed to spark honest conversation, spiritual reflection, and practical application

- At-Work Challenge: A relational or spiritual action step to take during the week

- Communication Framework: Tools to help you build trust, ask deeper questions, and disciple others naturally.

You'll meet once a week for about 60 minutes. Each session includes:

- A brief check-in: Where did you see God at work this week?

- A guided discussion around the weekly theme

- A closing prayer and challenge for the week ahead

If You're Leading a Group

You don't need to be a pastor or teacher. You just need a willing heart and a commitment to create space for others to grow.

This guide includes:

- Tips for facilitating discussion
- Tools for building trust and transparency
- Weekly prompts and communication templates
- A simple framework for launching and multiplying your group

If You're Joining a Group

Come ready to grow. This study isn't about checking boxes, it's about transformation.

You'll be challenged to:

- Reflect on your faith and leadership
- Build deeper relationships with other people
- Take action in your workplace that reflects Jesus' love and truth

You don't need to prepare anything in advance. Just show up, be honest, and let God work.

HOW TO LEAD A GROUP

Note for Pastors and Ministry Leaders:

If you're using this guide to disciple staff, volunteers, or high-capacity leaders, this section provides a simple framework you can use to train facilitators. Whether you're leading a group yourself or equipping others to do so, the principles here will help foster trust, transparency, and spiritual depth.

You don't need to be a pastor, teacher, or expert to lead this study. You just need a willing heart and a commitment to create space where people can grow spiritually, relationally, and professionally.

This guide gives you everything you need to lead with confidence:

- Weekly themes and discussion questions
- At-work challenges to apply faith
- Tools to foster trust, curiosity, and discipleship
- Communication prompts deepen relationships

Your role isn't to teach, it's to facilitate. That means guiding conversation, modeling vulnerability, and helping people connect their faith to their work.

Weekly Session Structure

Each session is designed to create space for God to move through scripture, story, and shared experience. Whether you're leading in a church, workplace, or community setting, this rhythm helps build trust, foster discipleship, and activate faith in real time.

Total Time: 60 Minutes

1. Check-In (5–10 min)

Start with this grounding question:

"Where did you see God at work this week?"

This opens the door to reflection and sets the tone for spiritual depth. Use the communication framework to guide this moment, especially the first two steps: sharing history and mentoring.

2. Discussion (35-45 min)

Walk through the weekly theme using the provided questions.

- Don't rush.
- Pause when the Holy Spirit prompts deeper conversation.
- Tie the discussion back to the week's scripture and real-life application.
- Encourage vulnerability and curiosity.

3. Wrap-Up (5-10 min)

- Summarize key insights
- Assign the at-work challenge
- Encourage midweek connection
- Close in prayer

Midweek Rhythm

To keep the study alive between sessions:

- Send a Wednesday message with the week's theme, scripture, and a reflection prompt

- Encourage 1:1 conversations or check-ins

- Celebrate small wins and spiritual growth

- Use the communication framework to deepen relationships

Facilitator's Role

You're not here to teach—you're here to create space.

- Model vulnerability

- Ask layered questions

- Guide transitions with spiritual attentiveness

- Make sure every person feels seen, heard, and challenged

Practice active listening.

- Paraphrase what someone shares to show you're tracking. Affirm their courage. Guide the group forward.

- Share your own story. Vulnerability invites vulnerability. Share enough to open the door, then step back and let others walk through it.

Manage group dynamics.

- Redirect dominant voices with grace: "Thanks for sharing, let's hear from someone else."

- Invite quieter participants: "[Name], I'd love to hear your thoughts."

- Gently guide emotional moments: "Thank you for trusting us. Let's focus on one part of that story."

Go get everyone.

- No one should leave unseen.

- Your goal each week is to create space where every person feels known and challenged.

Spiritual Preparation

Before you lead others, lead yourself into the presence of God.

Each week:

- Pray for your group by name

- Reflect on the theme personally

- Release distractions and ask for discernment

- Trust the Holy Spirit to do the deeper work

You're not just running a meeting. You're hosting a sacred space where people encounter Jesus.

Multiplying the Movement

After completing the study, invite others to lead. Share your experience. Offer support. Encourage them to use this guide to start their own group.

This is how the movement grows. One person, one group, one workplace at a time.

This rhythm is simple, repeatable, and powerful.

It's not about perfection, it's about presence.

Let God do the deeper work.

LAUNCHING A GROUP IN YOUR CHURCH OR WORKPLACE

Whether you're a pastor discipling staff or church leaders, or a Christian leader starting a group in your office, this guide is built for easy implementation and spiritual depth. You don't need a seminary degree or a ministry budget, just a clear invitation, a few committed people, and a willingness to lead with authenticity.

For Pastors and Ministry Leaders

This study is a powerful tool for discipling high-capacity people—staff, volunteers, donors, or business leaders in your congregation. It's designed to:

- Deepen spiritual maturity beyond Sunday

- Equip people to lead in their workplaces with integrity and faith

- Multiply discipleship through mentorship and small group leadership

- How to Start:

- Hand-select 6–12 people who show leadership, curiosity, and relational strength

- Walk through the 10-week study together

- Use the guide to train future facilitators and expand the ministry organically

- Support leaders with weekly encouragement and spiritual coaching

This is a scalable model for spiritual formation, one that builds trust, fosters transformation, and multiplies impact.

For Marketplace Leaders

You don't need permission to start a group. You just need a calling and this guide.

Whether you're a business owner, executive, team leader, or trusted colleague, you can create a space where faith and work intersect. This study gives you the tools to:

- Invite others into honest, faith-centered conversation
- Lead weekly sessions with confidence
- Build trust and transparency in your workplace
- Multiply the movement by equipping others to lead

How to Start:

1. Pray and prepare. Ask God to show you who to invite.

2. Choose a time and place. Lunch hour, early morning, virtual, whatever works.

3. Use the guide. Follow the weekly rhythm, lean into the questions, and let God lead.

You'll be surprised how quickly trust grows and how powerfully God moves when people bring Jesus to work.

WEEKLY SESSIONS

WEEK ONE: BUILDING AUTHENTIC RELATIONSHIPS AT WORK

Theme: Trust is the foundation of spiritual leadership.

Scripture Focus:

1 Thessalonians 2:8: "Because we loved you so much, we were delighted to share with you not only the gospel of God but our lives as well."

Proverbs 27:17: "As iron sharpens iron, so one person sharpens another."

John 15:15: "I no longer call you servants… Instead, I have called you friends."

Romans 12:10: "Be devoted to one another in love. Honor one another above yourselves."

Proverbs 17:17: "A friend loves at all times, and a brother is born for a time of adversity."

Colossians 3:23–24: "Whatever you do, work at it with all your heart, as working for the Lord, not for human masters…"

Why This Matters

Most people don't struggle with knowing what's right—they struggle with knowing who's safe. In the workplace, relationships often stay surface-level: efficient, polite, and professional. But spiritual leadership requires something deeper.

Jesus didn't disciple from a distance. He walked with people. He asked questions. He shared meals. He told stories. He invited others into His life.

If we want to lead spiritually at work, we must start by building trust. That means showing up with authenticity, listening with curiosity, and sharing our stories, not just our strategies.

Icebreaker: Modeling Curiosity and Connection through Your Story

This week, we begin with the first two steps of our communication framework:

1.   Be Curious About Others

2.   Tell Your Story

Invite each participant to introduce themselves briefly, sharing both spiritual and vocational background.

"Let's go around the room and share briefly. Keep it to about a minute each. I'll start."

Icebreaker Questions:

- What's your name, and how long have you been connected to a faith community or a group that's helped you grow spiritually?

- What do you do for work or vocation right now?

- What drew you to this small group study and what were you hoping to explore or experience?

- How would you describe your relationship with God right now or your journey with Him over time? (Encourage honesty, not perfection.)

- Do you feel like you bring Jesus into your work today? If so, how? If not, what makes that hard?

Teaching Moment: The Communication Framework and The Four Spaces of Belonging

After introductions, take a few minutes to teach the Communication Framework (found in the appendix) and the Four Spaces of Belonging. These help people conceptually understand how relationships grow (Four Spaces) while providing tactical steps (Communication Framework) to grow new relationships out of thin air.

The eight steps in the Communication Framework are:

Step 1: Be curious about someone else's story

Step 2: Tell your personal story

Step 3: Seek counsel

Step 4: Invite someone you don't know well to coffee

Step 5: Search for a mentor

Step 6: Become a mentor

Step 7: Explore spiritual openness at work

Step 8: Ask about someone's faith history

"We all live in different relational spaces. In this group, we want to move intentionally, from surface-level connection to spiritual depth. How do we make that relational movement? Let's talk about the four kinds of relationship spaces."

The Four Spaces:

- Public: Surface connections, like attending a work event or cheering for a team

- Social: Neighborly acts, like helping a colleague with a task

- Personal: Close friendships sharing challenges, like family or work struggles

- Intimate: Rare, deep bonds with a few (e.g., spouse, mentor) where you share vulnerable thoughts and faith

"This week, we practiced the first two steps of our communication framework:

1. Be curious about others

2. Tell your story

These are the building blocks of trust. When we ask someone about their story and respond with our own, we earn the right to move from social to personal, and sometimes even to intimacy."

Group DNA:

In this group, we operate in love, with transparency, and with a shared goal: to move from public to social to personal—and to risk intimacy with other people.

That's where transformation happens.

Group Discussion

"Now that we understand the concept (Four Spaces), let's practice with the tactics (Communication Framework)." Use these questions to guide deeper conversation. Let the Spirit lead.

1. What does "authenticity" mean to you in a work setting?

2. Where do you feel most known, or most unknown, at work?

3. What holds you back from being more open or honest with others?

4. How do you think trust is built in a professional environment?

5. What would it look like to lead with authenticity this week?

Relational Challenge: Steps 1 & 2

Be Curious About Others & Tell Your Story

This week, practice both steps in tandem:

- Ask someone at work or in your group about their story: faith, work, or life
- Then share a part of your own story that connects to theirs

This isn't about performance. It's about presence.

Curiosity builds safety. Vulnerability builds trust. Together, they open the door to discipleship.

Midweek Message

Theme: Authentic Relationships

Scripture: 1 Thessalonians 2:8

Reflection: Where do you feel most known at work? Where do you feel most hidden?

Relational Challenge: Be curious about someone's story. Ask a colleague how long they've worked there, what they do, or what drew them to the role. Then share a part of your own story that connects.

Closing Comments

This week, we got to know each other. That's the first step in building spiritual trust.

Step one in our communication framework is to be curious about others. When we ask someone about their story, and respond with part of our own, we begin to move from surface connection to deeper spiritual depth.

Your homework this week is simple: be curious. Ask someone you don't know well about their work story. How long have they been there? What do they do? What do they care about?

Then, if the moment feels right, share something that connects. That's how trust grows and how Jesus shows up at work.

Closing Prayer

"God, thank You for the people You've placed in our lives and workplaces. Give us the courage to lead with authenticity, to share our stories, and to build trust that reflects Your love. Help us see others the way You see them and to be seen ourselves. Amen."

WEEK TWO: WISDOM IN DECISION-MAKING

Theme: God's wisdom is available, and it transforms how we lead, decide, and respond at work.

> **Scripture Focus:**
>
> James 1:5: "If any of you lacks wisdom, you should ask God, who gives generously to all without finding fault…"
>
> Proverbs 3:5–6: "Trust in the Lord with all your heart and lean not on your own understanding…"
>
> Colossians 1:9: "…that you may be filled with the knowledge of His will in all spiritual wisdom and understanding."
>
> Psalm 32:8: "I will instruct you and teach you in the way you should go…"

God at Work Reflection

Leader Prompt:

"Before we jump into today's theme, let's start with a question we'll ask every week:

Where did you see God at work this week?

It could be something at work, at home, in a conversation, or even in a moment of challenge. Let's take a few minutes to share."

Relational Debrief (from Week 1)

"Last week, we practiced being curious about others, asking about their story, role, or what they care about.

Did anyone get a chance to try that? What happened? Was it good, awkward, surprising, encouraging?

And as you reflect…

Where did you see God show up in that moment—or in what you learned from it?"

Affirm effort, not outcomes. Celebrate curiosity and presence.

Why This Matters

Every person faces decisions at work, some tactical, some relational, some deeply personal. But few pause to ask: What does wisdom look like here?

God's wisdom isn't just for church or crisis. His wisdom is for contracts, meetings, hiring, strategy, and conflict. It's available, practical, and transformative.

This week, we will explore how to seek wisdom and how sharing our decision-making process can build trust and spiritual depth with others.

Opening Reflection

"Think about a decision you've made recently at work, big or small. What influenced it? What voices did you listen to? Did you invite God into it?"

Let a few participants share briefly. Then transition into the group discussion.

Group Discussion

Do you have mentors at work? How do you seek wisdom in business decisions?

> Share a time you made a poor decision without counsel. What happened?
>
> Share a time you avoided a bad decision because of good counsel. What made that counsel trustworthy?
>
> How do you find wise counselors in your life?
>
> How do you discern when God is speaking through someone?
>
> What does it look like to "carry each other's burdens" in a professional setting?

Tell Your Story

Last week, we practiced being curious about others. This week, we take the next step: sharing our own story.

"When we share our story - especially around real decisions - we invite others into our process. It's not about having all the answers. It's about modeling humility, faith, and transparency."

Relational Challenge: Step 2 of 8

Tell Your Story

This week, look for a moment to share part of your decision-making story with someone at work:

- A challenge you faced
- A moment of prayer or counsel
- A lesson learned
- Provides the details as well as your feeling about the moment

You're not preaching. You're modeling.

When you share your story, you give others permission to reflect on theirs.

Midweek Message

Theme: Wisdom in Decision Making

Scripture: James 1:5

Reflection: Where do you need wisdom this week? Who could you invite into that process?

Relational Challenge: Tell your story. Share a moment when you wrestled with a decision and how you sought wisdom.

Closing Comments

This week, we're learning to lead with wisdom and to share our process with others.

Step two in our communication framework is to tell our story. When you share how you've wrestled with a decision, you model humility and faith. You build trust. You open the door to spiritual conversation.

Your homework: Look for a moment to share a decision-making story with someone at work. It doesn't have to be dramatic, just real.

Closing Prayer

"God, thank You for being generous with Your wisdom. Help us seek You in our decisions and share our stories with courage and humility. May our choices reflect Your heart and invite others to know You more. Amen."

WEEK THREE: INTEGRITY AND ETHICS IN BUSINESS

Theme: Integrity isn't just about avoiding wrongdoing—it's about aligning our decisions with God's character.

> **Scripture Focus:**
>
> Proverbs 11:3: "The integrity of the upright guides them, but the unfaithful are destroyed by their duplicity."
>
> Psalm 15:1–2: "Lord, who may dwell in your sacred tent? … The one whose walk is blameless, who does what is righteous…"
>
> Titus 2:7: "In everything set them an example by doing what is good. In your teaching show integrity, seriousness…"
>
> Proverbs 13:20: "Walk with the wise and become wise, for a companion of fools suffers harm."

God at Work Reflection

Leader Prompt:

"Before we jump into today's theme, let's start with our weekly question:

Where did you see God at work this week?

It could be something at work, at home, in a conversation, or even in a moment of challenge. Let's take a few minutes to share."

Relational Debrief (from Week 2)

"Last week, we practiced telling our story, especially around a decision we've made. Did anyone get a chance to share a moment of wrestling or wisdom with someone at work? What happened? Was it good, awkward, surprising, encouraging?

How might it be possible that God was in that moment?

Maybe in the timing, the courage to speak, the way someone responded, or what it revealed about you."

Normalize imperfect attempts. Celebrate courage and connection.

Why This Matters

Work is full of ethical gray zones, moments where character is tested, shortcuts are tempting, and silence feels safer than truth. Integrity isn't just about what we avoid, it's about who we become.

God calls us to be people of integrity: consistent, trustworthy, and anchored in His truth. But we don't walk that path alone. Seeking counsel, inviting wise voices into our decisions, is part of how we grow.

This week, we will explore how to lead with integrity and how asking for input can deepen trust and spiritual connection.

Opening Reflection

"Think about a time when you faced an ethical decision at work. What helped you choose the right path or what made it hard?"

Let a few participants share briefly. Then transition into the group discussion.

> **Group Discussion**
>
> 1. What does integrity look like in your current role or industry?
>
> 2. Where do you feel most tempted to compromise—or stay silent?
>
> 3. Who do you trust to speak the truth into your life when things get messy?
>
> 4. How do you typically respond when someone challenges your thinking or behavior?
>
> 5. What would it look like to seek counsel more intentionally this week?

Teaching Moment: Step 3 of the Communication Framework

Seek Counsel

"Integrity grows in community. When we invite others into our decision-making - especially around ethical challenges - we model humility and build trust."

Encourage participants to reflect on who they turn to for wisdom. Then ask:

- Who's someone you've sought counsel from in the past?
- What made that person trustworthy?
- Is there someone you need to reach out to this week?

Relational Challenge: Step 3 of 8

This week, identify one decision, challenge, or tension at work and ask someone you trust for input. It could be:

- A colleague

- A mentor
- A friend in this group

You're not asking them to fix it. You're inviting them to walk with you.

Midweek Message

Theme: Integrity and Ethics

Scripture: Proverbs 11:3

Reflection: Where are you tempted to compromise this week? Who could you invite into that moment?

Relational Challenge: Seek counsel. Ask someone you trust for input on a decision or challenge.

Closing Comments

This week, we're leaning into integrity, not just as a moral stance, but as a spiritual posture.

Step three in our communication framework is to seek counsel. When we ask for wisdom, we model humility. We build trust. We grow.

Your homework: Identify one decision or challenge at work and ask someone you trust for input.

Let God speak through others.

Closing Prayer

"God, thank You for being our guide and our source of truth. Help us walk with integrity, seek wise counsel, and lead in a way that reflects Your heart. Give us courage to ask for help—and humility to receive it. Amen."

WEEK FOUR: HARD WORK AND DILIGENCE

Theme: Our work ethic reflects our worship. Diligence isn't just about effort. It's about spiritual integrity.

> **Scripture Focus:**
>
> Colossians 3:23–24: "Whatever you do, work at it with all your heart, as working for the Lord…"
>
> Proverbs 12:11: "Those who work their land will have abundant food…"
>
> 2 Thessalonians 3:10: "…The one who is unwilling to work shall not eat."
>
> Ecclesiastes 9:10: "Whatever your hand finds to do, do it with all your might…"

God at Work Reflection

Leader Prompt:

"Before we jump into today's theme, let's start with our weekly question:

Where did you see God at work this week?

It could be something at work, at home, in a conversation, or even in a moment of challenge. Let's take a few minutes to share."

Relational Debrief (from Week 3)

"Last week, we practiced seeking counsel—inviting someone into a decision or challenge.

Did anyone get a chance to ask for input from someone they trust? What happened? What did you learn?"

How might it be possible that God was in that moment?

Maybe in the timing, the courage to ask, the wisdom received, or the way it shaped your next step.

Affirm humility and courage. Normalize imperfect attempts.

Why This Matters

Work is sacred. It's not just a means to an end, it's a place where character is revealed, relationships are built, and God is present.

Diligence isn't just about working hard, it's about working with integrity, consistency, and purpose. When we show up fully, we reflect the image of a God who never cuts corners.

This week, we explore how spiritual leadership includes work ethic and how inviting someone to coffee can be a simple act of relational diligence.

Opening Reflection

"Think about someone at work who consistently shows up with excellence. What makes them stand out?

Now think about your own work. Where do you feel most diligent? Where do you feel distracted or disengaged?"

Let a few participants share. Then transition to group discussion.

> **Group Discussion**
>
> 1. What does "working as unto the Lord" mean in your current role?
>
> 2. Where do you feel most tempted to coast, cut corners, or disengage?
>
> 3. How does your work ethic impact your witness?
>
> 4. Who's someone at work you admire and what could you learn from them?
>
> 5. What would it look like to pursue relational diligence this week?

Relational Challenge: Step 4 of 8

Inviting Someone to Coffee

This week, take one small step of relational diligence:

- Invite someone you don't know well to coffee, lunch, or a walk
- Use the time to ask about their role, story, or perspective

You're not trying to "go deep". You're showing up with intentionality.

That's how trust begins.

Midweek Message

Theme: Hard Work and Diligence

Scripture: Colossians 3:23

Reflection: Where do you feel most engaged at work and where do you feel most checked out?

Relational Challenge: Invite someone to coffee. Ask about their role, their story, or what they enjoy about their work.

Closing Comments

This week, we're connecting diligence to discipleship.

Step four in our communication framework is to invite someone to coffee. It's a simple act but it carries spiritual weight.

Your homework: identify someone you don't know well and invite them to connect. Ask about their work, their story, or what they care about.

That's how we move from public to personal and how Jesus shows up in everyday moments.

Closing Prayer

"God, thank You for the work You've given us and the people You've placed around us. Help us show up with excellence, integrity, and care. Give us courage to reach out, and wisdom to build trust. Amen."

WEEK FIVE: COMMUNICATION AND LISTENING

Theme: Listening is leadership. The way we communicate reflects the way we value others and the way we follow Christ.

> **Scripture Focus:**
>
> James 1:19: "Everyone should be quick to listen, slow to speak and slow to become angry."
>
> Proverbs 18:13: "To answer before listening—that is folly and shame."
>
> Ecclesiastes 5:2: "Do not be quick with your mouth… let your words be few."
>
> Proverbs 20:5: "The purposes of a person's heart are deep waters, but one who has insight draws them out."

God at Work Reflection

Leader Prompt:

"Before we jump into today's theme, let's start with our weekly question:

Where did you see God at work this week?

It could be something at work, at home, in a conversation, or even in a moment of challenge. Let's take a few minutes to share."

Relational Debrief (from Week 4)

"Last week, we practiced relational diligence by inviting someone to coffee.

Did anyone get a chance to reach out to someone new? What did you learn about them or about yourself?"

How might it be possible that God was in that moment?

Maybe in the timing, the courage to reach out, the openness of the conversation, or what it revealed about your role."

Affirm intentionality. Celebrate small steps toward deeper connection.

Why This Matters

Most workplace communication is transactional, focused on speed, clarity, and control. But spiritual leadership requires something deeper: listening with empathy, speaking with wisdom, and creating space for others to be known.

Jesus asked questions. He listened. He responded with truth and grace.

This week, we explore how communication becomes discipleship and how pursuing a mentor can help us grow in both clarity and humility.

Opening Reflection

"Think about someone who listens well—someone who makes you feel heard. What do they do differently?"

Let a few participants share. Then transition to group discussion.

> **Group Discussion**
>
> 1. What's one area of communication you struggle with—listening, clarity, tone, timing?
>
> 2. How do you typically respond when someone shares something vulnerable or difficult?
>
> 3. What does it look like to listen spiritually—not just professionally?
>
> 4. Who's someone you admire for their wisdom or presence?
>
> 5. What would it look like to ask them for guidance or mentorship?

Relational Challenge: Step 5 of 8

Search for a Mentor

This week, take a step toward growth:

- Identify someone you admire for their wisdom, character, or spiritual maturity

- Reach out and ask for a conversation—about work, life, or faith

- This is different from step three when you were seeking counsel on a single item or element of your work. Search out a true mentor across multiple elements of your work or personal life and ask to meet with them regularly.

You're not asking for a lifelong commitment. You're opening the door to guidance.

Midweek Message

Theme: Communication and Listening

Scripture: James 1:19

Reflection: Where do you need to slow down and listen this week? Who could help you grow in that area?

Relational Challenge: Seek out a mentor. Ask someone you respect to meet with you regularly in a mentorship role.

Closing Comments

This week, we're learning that communication is more than clarity, it's connection.

Step five in our communication framework is to search for a mentor. When we ask for guidance, we model humility and pursue growth.

Your homework: identify someone you admire and ask for a conversation. It could be about work, faith, or life.

That's how discipleship begins, one question at a time.

Closing Prayer

"God, thank You for the people You've placed around us. Help us listen well, speak wisely, and pursue growth with humility. Give us courage to ask for guidance and grace to receive it. Amen."

WEEK SIX: RESILIENCE AND ADAPTABILITY

Theme: Resilience isn't just about surviving—it's about growing through challenge and helping others do the same.

> **Scripture Focus:**
>
> Romans 5:3–4: "…suffering produces perseverance; perseverance, character; and character, hope."
>
> James 1:2–4: "Consider it pure joy… whenever you face trials… because you know that the testing of your faith produces perseverance."
>
> 2 Corinthians 4:8–9: "We are hard pressed on every side, but not crushed…"
>
> Galatians 6:2: "Carry each other's burdens, and in this way you will fulfill the law of Christ."

God at Work Reflection

Leader Prompt:

"Before we jump into today's theme, let's start with our weekly question:

Where did you see God at work this week?

It could be something at work, at home, in a conversation, or even in a moment of challenge. Let's take a few minutes to share."

Relational Debrief (from Week 5)

"Last week, we practiced searching for a mentor, someone we admire and could learn from.

Did anyone reach out for a conversation? What did you learn or what held you back?"

How might it be possible that God was in that moment?

Celebrate initiative. Normalize hesitation. Affirm the value of asking.

Why This Matters

Resilience is forged in adversity, but it's multiplied through community.

When we adapt, endure, and grow, we don't just strengthen ourselves, we become a source of strength for others.

Spiritual leadership means showing up in hard seasons and helping others do the same. This week, we explore how becoming a mentor is an act of resilience and discipleship.

Opening Reflection

"Think about a time when you faced a challenge at work. Who helped you through it or who watched you grow?"

Let a few participants share. Then transition to group discussion.

Group Discussion

1. What's one challenge you've faced recently—and how did you respond?

2. Where do you feel stretched or tested in your current role?

3. Who's someone you've helped through a tough season?

4. What does spiritual resilience look like in your workplace?

> 5. What would it look like to mentor someone through a challenge?

Relational Challenge: Step 6 of 8

Become a Mentor

This week, take a step toward spiritual multiplication:

- Identify someone who might benefit from your experience
- Reach out with encouragement, support, or an offer to connect

You're not committing to a formal role, you're opening the door to discipleship.

Midweek Message

Theme: Resilience and Adaptability

Scripture: Romans 5:3–4

Reflection: Where have you grown through challenge—and who could benefit from that growth?

Relational Challenge: Seek counsel. Ask someone you trust for input on a decision or challenge.

Closing Comments

This week, we're learning that resilience isn't just personal, it's relational.

Step six in our communication framework is to become a mentor. When we invest in others, we multiply strength, wisdom, and hope.

Your homework: identify someone who might benefit from your experience and reach out. It could be a word of encouragement, a shared story, or an offer to connect.

That's how discipleship grows, through presence, not perfection.

Closing Prayer

"God, thank You for walking with us through every challenge. Help us grow in resilience and help us multiply it by investing in others. Give us eyes to see who needs encouragement, and hearts willing to respond. Amen."

WEEK SEVEN: FINANCIAL RESPONSIBILITY, STEWARDSHIP, AND GENEROSITY

Theme: Stewardship is spiritual leadership. How we handle money reflects what we value—and who we trust.

Scripture Focus:

Matthew 6:24: "You cannot serve both God and money."

Proverbs 3:9: "Honor the Lord with your wealth…"

1 Timothy 6:17–19: "…be rich in good deeds, generous and willing to share."

Luke 16:10: "Whoever can be trusted with very little can also be trusted with much…"

God at Work Reflection

Leader Prompt:

"Before we jump into today's theme, let's start with our weekly question:

Where did you see God at work this week?

It could be something at work, at home, in a conversation, or even in a moment of challenge. Let's take a few minutes to share."

Relational Debrief (from Week 6)

"Last week, we practiced becoming a mentor—investing in someone who might benefit from our experience.

Did anyone get a chance to reach out or encourage someone? What happened? Was it good, awkward, surprising, encouraging?

How might it be possible that God was in that moment?

Maybe in the courage to speak, the timing of the conversation, the openness of the other person, or the clarity it gave you."

Affirm presence over perfection. Celebrate spiritual awareness and relational investment.

Why This Matters

God cares deeply about how we handle money.

Stewardship isn't just about giving. It's about trust, integrity, and generosity. But it's also bigger than money.

We've been entrusted with time, talents, and treasures and all three are spiritual resources.

- Time: How we show up, prioritize, and invest in others
- Talents: The skills, wisdom, and experience we've gained
- Treasures: The financial resources we manage and share

Stewardship means using all of these with purpose.

It's not just about what we give, it's about how we lead, how we trust, and how we reflect God's character in every decision.

Opening Reflection

"Think about a financial decision you've made at work—big or small. What influenced it? What values were at play?"

Let a few participants share. Then transition to group discussion.

> **Group Discussion**
>
> 1. What's one financial decision you've made recently and what shaped it?
>
> 2. Where do you feel tension between generosity and control?
>
> 3. How does your financial stewardship reflect your spiritual values?
>
> 4. Who's someone you admire for how they handle money and what have you learned from them?
>
> 5. What would it look like to explore spiritual openness at work through financial integrity or generosity?

RELATIONAL CHALLENGE: STEP 7 OF 8

Explore Spiritual Openness at Work

This week, take a step toward spiritual leadership:

Explore your work policies toward faith. Many Christians feel they must firewall their faith at work though most organizations openly embrace diversity.

Look for a moment to model generosity, integrity, or humility in a financial decision

If the moment feels right, ask a colleague how they think about generosity or stewardship

You're not trying to "go deep"—you're creating space for spiritual openness.

Midweek Message

Theme: Financial Stewardship

Scripture: Proverbs 3:9

Reflection: Where are you being invited to trust God financially this week?

Relational Challenge: Explore spiritual openness at work. Model generosity or integrity and ask someone how they think about stewardship.

Closing Comments

This week, we're learning that stewardship is spiritual leadership.

Step seven in our communication framework is to explore spiritual openness at work. When we handle money with integrity and generosity, we reflect God's character, and we open the door to meaningful conversation.

Your homework: look for a moment to model financial stewardship. If the moment feels right, ask someone how they think about generosity or trust.

Closing Prayer

"God, thank You for entrusting us with resources. Help us handle money with wisdom, humility, and generosity. Show us how to reflect Your character in our decisions and how to invite others into spiritual openness. Amen."

WEEK EIGHT: MENTORSHIP AND DISCIPLESHIP IN THE WORKPLACE

Theme: Investing in Others for Growth and Glory

Scripture Focus:

Proverbs 27:17: "As iron sharpens iron, so one person sharpens another."

2 Timothy 2:2: "Entrust to reliable people who will also be qualified to teach others."

Matthew 5:16: "Let your light shine before others…"

Titus 2:3–5: "Teach the older… [to] urge the younger…"

Proverbs 13:20: "Walk with the wise and become wise."

Matthew 28:19–20: "Go and make disciples… teaching them to obey everything I have commanded you."

God at Work Reflection

Leader Prompt:

"Before we jump into today's theme, let's start with our weekly question:

Where did you see God at work this week?

It could be something at work, at home, in a conversation, or even in a moment of challenge. Let's take a few minutes to share."

Relational Debrief (from Week 7)

"Last week, we practiced exploring spiritual openness at work especially through how we handle resources.

What HR policies did you discover at work? What does that mean for you?

Did anyone get a chance to model generosity or integrity—or ask someone how they think about stewardship? What happened? Good, awkward, surprising, encouraging?

How might it be possible that God was in that moment?

Maybe in the courage to ask, the response you received, or the clarity it gave you."

Affirm spiritual courage. Celebrate relational movement and leadership growth.

Why This Matters

Mentorship and discipleship are the heartbeat of spiritual multiplication.

They're not just about transferring skills. They're about shaping character, deepening faith, and building trust.

The workplace is full of opportunities to invest in others.

When we mentor with intention and disciple with humility, we reflect Christ and we build a culture of growth and glory.

Opening Reflection

"Think about someone who mentored you at work or in faith. What did they do that made a lasting impact?"

Let a few participants share. Then transition to group discussion.

Group Discussion

1. What do these Scriptures teach us about our influence and responsibility toward others at work?

2. How does entrusting wisdom to others relate to mentorship in a professional setting?

3. Why is making disciples relevant to the workplace and what does walking-with-the-wise look like there?

4. What unique opportunities or challenges have you faced mentoring at work?

5. What practical steps can you take to build a culture of discipleship in your workplace?

Teaching Moment: Multiplication Through Mentorship

"Mentorship goes beyond skill, also covering character, faith, and intentional investment.

Discipleship is the spiritual extension of mentorship. It's how we multiply what God has taught us."

Share a personal story or example:

- A time you were mentored through failure or growth
- A moment when you mentored someone and saw spiritual fruit
- How intentional investment deepened relational trust

Relational Challenge: Multiply Through Mentorship

This week, take a step toward spiritual multiplication:

- Initiate a mentorship conversation
- Reach out to someone to offer guidance—or seek it

- Continue incorporating faith elements into your work life
- Journal the outcome and how it builds intentional relationships

Midweek Message

Theme: Mentorship and Discipleship

Scripture: 2 Timothy 2:2

Reflection: Who's someone you could invest in this week—professionally or spiritually?

Relational Challenge: Seek someone you can mentor. Respond to the call to pay forward the knowledge and experience you have experienced.

Closing Comments

This week, we're learning that mentorship and discipleship are how the movement continues.

When we invest in others, we multiply impact. We sharpen character. We reflect Christ.

Your homework: Initiate a mentorship conversation. Offer guidance. Seek wisdom. Build intentional relationships that reflect spiritual leadership.

Closing Prayer

"Lord, give us courage to disciple and wisdom to mentor. Help us multiply what You've taught us and invest in others for Your glory. Amen."

WEEK NINE: HANDLING STRESS, BURNOUT, AND TEMPTATIONS AT WORK

Theme: Finding Rest and Resistance at Work Through Faith

Scripture Focus:

Matthew 11:28–30: "Come to me, all you who are weary and burdened, and I will give you rest."

Philippians 4:6–7: "Do not be anxious about anything… and the peace of God… will guard your hearts and your minds."

1 Corinthians 10:13: "No temptation… [is] beyond what you can bear… [God] will provide a way out."

James 1:2–4: "Consider it pure joy… because the testing of your faith produces perseverance."

Psalm 55:22: "Cast your cares on the Lord and he will sustain you."

Isaiah 40:31: "Those who hope in the Lord will renew their strength."

Proverbs 3:5–6: "Trust in the Lord with all your heart… and he will make your paths straight."

God at Work Reflection

Leader Prompt:

"Before we dive into today's theme, let's begin with our weekly rhythm:

Where did you see God at work this week?

It could be in a conversation, a moment of clarity, a challenge, or a small act of courage. Let's take a few minutes to share."

Relational Debrief (from Week 8)

"Last week, we practiced mentorship and discipleship, investing in others for growth and glory.

Did anyone get a chance to initiate a mentorship conversation or offer guidance? What happened? Was it encouraging, awkward, surprising?

How might it be possible that God was in that moment?

Maybe in the courage to reach out, the timing of the conversation, or the trust built."

Affirm spiritual leadership. Celebrate relational movement and intentional investment.

Why This Matters

Stress, burnout, and temptation are part of every workplace.

But they don't have to define our story.

God offers us rest in the middle of pressure, strength in the face of temptation, and peace that surpasses understanding.

This week, we explore how to respond to workplace stress and spiritual struggle, not with escape, but with faith, community, and resilience.

Opening Reflection

"Think about a time when you felt overwhelmed at work by pressure, fatigue, or temptation.

What did you do? Where did you turn?"

Let a few participants share. Then transition into Scripture and discussion.

> **Group Discussion**
>
> 1. How do these Scriptures offer rest from stress and burnout?
>
> 2. What assurances do they give us when facing temptation?
>
> 3. Why is trusting God essential when navigating workplace pressure?
>
> 4. Which verse speaks most directly to your current season and why?

Teaching Moment: Rest and Resistance

"Stress and temptation are real and so is God's provision.

We're not called to power through, but we are called to abide.

When we bring our burdens to God, He doesn't just remove them, He strengthens us to walk through them."

Share a personal story of burnout, temptation, or pressure:

- What triggered it
- How you responded
- Where God met you
- What changed in you or your relationships

Then invite the group to reflect:

- How does this story connect to the Scriptures we read?
- Can anyone share a moment when they experienced God's peace or strength in a stressful season at work?

Relational Challenge: Rest and Resistance

This week, take a step toward spiritual resilience:

- Identify a stressor or temptation you're facing
- Choose a Scripture to anchor you in that moment
- Share it with a trusted peer or mentor for encouragement and accountability
- Invite God into the pressure before it escalates

Midweek Message

Theme: Rest and Resistance

Scripture: Isaiah 40:31

Reflection: Where are you weary—and where do you need God's strength?

Relational Challenge: Name a stressor or temptation. Anchor yourself in Scripture. Invite someone to walk with you.

From Surface to Soul: Deeper Discussion Prompts

Facilitator Note: These prompts are designed to move from external stress to internal reflection. Use a gentle tone. Model vulnerability. Invite spiritual curiosity.

- What's been weighing on you lately at work?

- When you're under pressure, what temptations tend to surface—either in behavior or mindset?

- Can you recall a moment when you hit a wall, and God met you there? What shifted?

- Where do you tend to turn first when stress hits? Is it God, people, performance, escape? What does that reveal about your trust?

- What's one lie you've believed in moments of burnout or temptation? What truth from Scripture speaks directly to it?

- What's one step you can take this week to invite God into your stress or temptation before it escalates?

Closing Comments

This week check for stress triggers.

- Journal a plan using a Scripture for renewal

- Share it with a trusted peer for accountability

- Note where you see God's provision or peace

Closing Prayer

"Lord, grant us rest in our weariness, strength in our weakness, and victory in our trials. Help us trust You, lean on community, and reflect Your peace in our workplaces. May we be people of resilience, integrity, and grace. Amen."

WEEK TEN: LEGACY AND IMPACT AT WORK

Theme: Multiplying What Matters: Living and Leaving a Spiritual Legacy

Scripture Focus:

2 Timothy 4:7: "I have fought the good fight, I have finished the race, I have kept the faith."

Psalm 78:4: "We will tell the next generation the praiseworthy deeds of the Lord…"

Matthew 28:19–20: "Go and make disciples… teaching them to obey everything I have commanded you."

Proverbs 13:22: "A good person leaves an inheritance for their children's children…"

John 15:16: "I chose you and appointed you so that you might go and bear fruit, fruit that will last."

God at Work Reflection

Leader Prompt:

"Before we close out this series, let's begin with our weekly rhythm:

Where did you see God at work this week?

It could be in a conversation, a moment of clarity, a challenge, or a small act of courage. Let's take a few minutes to share."

Relational Debrief (from Week 9)

"Last week, we reflected on stress, burnout, and temptation—and how God meets us with rest and resistance.

Did anyone take a step to invite God into a pressure point? What happened—encouraging, surprising, clarifying?

How might it be possible that God was in that moment?

Maybe in the peace you felt, the conversation it opened, or the strength it gave you."

Affirm spiritual resilience. Celebrate movement toward trust, rest, and renewal.

Why This Matters

Legacy isn't just about what we leave behind, it's about what we multiply while we're here.

It's the fruit of intentional investment, spiritual courage, and relational trust.

This final session invites reflection on the full journey:

- What have you learned?
- What has shifted in you?
- Who will benefit from what God has done in your life?

Legacy is built, one conversation, one decision, one act of faith at a time.

Opening Reflection

"Think about someone whose legacy has shaped you spiritually, professionally, or relationally.

What did they do that left a lasting impact?"

Let a few participants share. Then transition into Scripture and discussion.

> **Group Discussion**
>
> 1. What do these Scriptures teach us about legacy and spiritual impact?
>
> 2. What kind of legacy do you want to leave at work, in your relationships, and in your faith?
>
> 3. Where have you seen fruit from the steps you've practiced in this series?
>
> 4. Who's someone you could invest in next—and what would that look like?
>
> 5. What's one way to keep this momentum going after the group ends?

Teaching Moment: Living a Legacy

"Legacy isn't built in one moment it's built through consistent faithfulness.

When we live with spiritual intention, we multiply impact.

When we disciple others, we extend the movement.

When we reflect Christ at work, we leave a trail of grace, truth, and transformation."

Group Discussion: Share a personal story:

- A moment when someone's legacy shaped your life

- A time when you saw spiritual fruit multiply through a simple act of obedience

- A reflection on what you hope your own legacy will be

- Invite the group to talk deeper about their legacy

Relational Challenge: Multiply the Movement

As we wrap up this study, act. This week, take a step toward legacy:

- Reflect on what you've learned over the past 10 weeks

- Identify one person you could invest in spiritually or professionally

- Share one insight, story, or Scripture that impacted you

- Invite them into a conversation, a challenge, or a next step

Final Challenge

- Reflect on your journey and journal what God has done

- Identify one person to invest in

- Share one insight or Scripture from this series

- Keep practicing the 8-Step Communication Framework

- Find other guys and duplicate this study with them – help others discover their journey with Christ

Closing Prayer

"Lord, thank You for the journey. Thank You for the growth, the courage, and the conversations. Help us carry this forward, multiplying what matters, investing in others, and reflecting Your love at work. May our legacy be one of grace, truth, and spiritual impact. Amen."

APPENDIX

8-STEP DISCIPLESHIP COMMUNICATION FRAMEWORK

Purpose:

To build authentic, Christ-centered relationships in the workplace through intentional conversation, vulnerability, and spiritual curiosity. These steps form a rhythm, not a checklist, for deepening trust, influence, and discipleship.

Step 1: Be curious about someone else's story

- Deepens connection through active listening

Step 2: Tell your personal story

- Build trust through vulnerability and shared experience

Step 3: Seek counsel

- Models humility and invites spiritual dialogue

Step 4: Invite someone you don't know well to coffee

- Expands relational reach and initiates new connections

Step 5: Search for a mentor

- Pursues growth through spiritual guidance

Step 6: Become a mentor

- Multiplies impact by investing in others

Step 7: Explore spiritual openness at work

- Engage culture with wisdom and initiative

Step 8: Ask about someone's faith history

- Invites spiritual depth through curiosity and care

These steps are introduced and practiced throughout the study.

They help us move from surface-level interactions to meaningful discipleship, one conversation at a time.

OUTCOME-BASED PROMOTIONAL MESSAGING FOR BRINGING JESUS TO WORK

Based on the book's vision of building a community of Christians who integrate faith into their workplaces through authentic, Christ-centered relationships and drawing from the heart of the study, rules of engagement (love, transparency, trust), and the Four Spaces of Belonging framework, I've crafted outcome-based promotional messaging.

This focuses on tangible results: transformed workplace relationships, broken barriers between faith and work, personal spiritual growth, and a multiplying discipleship impact. I've organized them into categories for easy use, such as taglines, social media posts, email blurbs, and website copy. Each emphasizes what participants will achieve, rather than just features.

Taglines (Short Headlines for Covers, Ads, or Banners)

- Transform Your Workplace: Move from Surface Chats to Soul-Deep Bonds, Integrating Faith Every Day.

- Break the Faith-Work Divide: Achieve Intimate, Christ-Centered Relationships That Spark Lasting Discipleship.

- Unlock Belonging at Work: Gain Trust, Transparency, and Transformation Through Jesus' Love.

- From Colleagues to Confidants: Build a Multiplying Movement of Faith-Fueled Connections.

- Experience Workplace Renewal: Foster Deep Intimacy with God and Others, One Space at a Time.

Social Media Posts (Ready-to-Post, with Hashtags for Engagement)

- Tired of keeping faith separate from your 9–5? 'Bringing Jesus to Work' equips you to build trust-based relationships that integrate Christ into every conversation—resulting in renewed purpose, deeper connections, and a discipleship ripple effect. Discover the Four Spaces of Belonging today! #FaithAtWork #ChristiansAtWork #DiscipleshipMovement

- Imagine turning casual office interactions into life-changing, faith-sharing moments. This study delivers: authentic bonds with colleagues, broken barriers between belief and business, and a community that multiplies God's love. Ready for transformation? #BringingJesusToWork #BelongingInBusiness

- Outcome: Stronger faith, closer workplace friends, and a legacy of discipleship. 'Bringing Jesus to Work' uses love, transparency, and the Four Spaces to guide you from public pleasantries to intimate spiritual growth. Who's joining the movement? #WorkplaceFaith #TrustAndTransparency

- Achieve what matters: Integrate Jesus into your career, foster vulnerability with peers, and ignite a chain of transformed lives. This isn't just a study—it's your path to meaningful impact at work. Link in bio! #ChristianLeadership #FourSpacesOfBelonging

Email Blurbs (For Newsletters or Invites, Focusing on Benefits)

- Subject: Revolutionize Your Work Life: Integrate Faith and Build Lasting Bonds Body: What if your workplace became a hub for Christ-centered growth? In *Bringing Jesus to Work*, you'll learn to navigate the Four Spaces of Belonging—Public, Social,

Personal, and Intimate—to create relationships rooted in love, transparency, and trust. The outcome? Deeper connections with colleagues, a seamless blend of faith and profession, and a multiplying discipleship movement that starts with you. Join Cohort One and see your career transformed. Sign up now!

- Subject: Break the Firewall: Faith-Infused Work Relationships Await Body: Struggling to bring Jesus into your daily grind? This study empowers you to practice curiosity, vulnerability, and transformation, leading to intimate, trust-based ties that honor God. Expect results like renewed workplace joy, authentic sharing of your faith journey, and a community that inspires others to follow. Don't miss out—experience the heart of discipleship at work!

Church Website Content Announcing the Study

- Discover the Power of Belonging: In a world where faith and work often feel worlds apart, *Bringing Jesus to Work* delivers a proven framework to bridge the gap. By embracing the Four Spaces of Belonging, you'll achieve intimate relationships with colleagues and God, fostering an environment of love, transparency, and trust. The real outcome? A transformed professional life where faith sparks daily decisions, challenges turn into opportunities for growth, and your influence multiplies through discipleship. Ideal for Christians ready to lead with Christ at the center—start your journey today and watch your workplace change.

- Outcome-Driven Faith Integration: Imagine ending the cultural firewall between your beliefs and your career. This study guides you through rules of engagement that build safe spaces for vulnerability, using the Four Spaces to progress from surface-level interactions to profound, faith-sharing bonds. You'll gain: Enhanced trust with team members, personal spiritual renewal, and the tools to launch a movement that disciples others.

Bringing Jesus to Work equips you for lasting impact—because when Jesus enters your workspace, everything elevates.